MW01245306

Laura grew up in Chicago, Illinois, but, since 1974, has spent most of her summers in St. Pete Beach, Florida. She earned her first BA from Columbia College, Chicago in English/creative writing. She subsequently earned her teaching degree from North Central College, Naperville, Illinois, then went on to earn an MAT from Aurora University, Aurora, Illinois. She is semi-retired, living in Florida full-time now after 20+ years of teaching mostly 4–5th grades, but she still teaches remotely. When she's not gardening, painting, reading, or cooking, she dips her toes in the surf and watches sunsets, birds, the stars, and writes. Of course! She is currently the Education Chair of St. Petersburg, Florida's chapter of Audubon Society.

For Katie, Johnny, and Mark

Laura DiMartino

SINGING DOWN THE RAIN

AUSTIN MACAULEY PUBLISHERS™

LONDON · CAMBRIDGE · NEW YORK · SHARJAH

Ordering Information
Quantity sales: Special discounts are available on quantity purchases by corporations, associations, and others. For details, contact the publisher at the address below.

Publisher's Cataloging-in-Publication data
DiMartino, Laura
Singing Down the Rain

ISBN 9781685627720 (Paperback)
ISBN 9781685627737 (Hardback)
ISBN 9781685627751 (ePub e-book)
ISBN 9781685627744 (Audiobook)

Library of Congress Control Number: 2023905983

www.austinmacauley.com/us

First Published 2023
Austin Macauley Publishers LLC
40 Wall Street, 33rd Floor, Suite 3302
New York, NY 10005
USA

mail-usa@austinmacauley.com
+1 (646) 5125767

Thanks to all my friends and family who have put up with my eccentricities over the years, especially: John DiMartino, John Jacob, John Wayne, Daniel McGivney, Chris Monroe, Deborah Ranieri-Banifazl, Margie Corp, Donza Ramos, Sandy Kolton-Applegate, Charis Look, Paul Hoover, Grant Hudson, Horatio Heck Montalvan, Courtney, Prentice, Wallace and William Melnyczenko.

A very special thank you, also, to the team at Austin Macauley.

Some of the poems in this book were previously published in three different magazines.

Table of Contents

I
Overtones

Finally

An old lady sits
next to me on the
Southwest plane to Tampa
contemplating a crossword,
gray curls reflecting smiles in
random time as she
carefully fits
the next word, letters looped
perfectly, into the
square boxes, and then,
stops her heart.

Back Room

She responds in
reflected hymns,
capturing old doubts as
seen in black and white films,
movies with the swagger and swirls
of evening gales and dust.
An owl twists her head, silently;
she mourns the loss of silver
light, clouds draped over a
gibbous waning moon. Whose face
would she sacrifice?
She's pulled apart,
bared with silent hands,
montage of grays and white,
a snowscape seen
out a window or
pictures foolishly taken,
returned without explanation,
so much frustration. Too much
to bear.
And she howls at the moon, and
the moon howls back.

Truth

Effortlessly
he binds her,
clouding the indigo sky with
breath, digressing the shadows,
fever climbing a ladder of hunger,
staccato rhythms on the timpani,
cacophony, slipping into fugue:
lost in blues, rhythm and blues.

Sweat, tears,
sharp cut of a knife.
In so deep,
it doesn't border on pain.
It does.

Gehenna

-1-

Ran that summer through the last
remaining forest sucking in
remnants of oxygen choking

greasy burns coating our skin,
coating our throats
our eyes narrow slits against
silted black sorrow that permutation

deer stumbling, my surprise
an otter one last beaver
squirrels I guess they never mattered but

some survived sprinting ahead as
fire chased our carbon stole our breath
us

never enough profit mining
chemical paper mineral
stripped down oil black
gold pumped

from her breast that
lady once worshiped grown
old in memory still quaking
still raped over

-3-

deserts in bloom with flowering
dust icicles drip north and south
currents codacide in
this; a new song just begun
without rhythm no beat
no dancing we made

one last polar bear

swim in vain

No Discussion

You wore your cap turned backward
in rebellion once, but what
you didn't seem to know
was the conformity it brought,
like ordinary uses for
extraordinary thought, like
the thin knife you used
as a lever against
the windowsill to uncork my
ten-dollar wine,

the way you
depleted a spot on your couch,
gave up a place you said was mine,
for a moment, anyway,
a moment, kind, when I believed
we'd become more than
friends, so

I must have lingered,
too many moments
sipping that cheap wine

watching vistas, sunrises,
technicolor sunsets drift
through my mind, while
you read the daily papers,
one at a time, blind
to my continued presence,
cap turned 'round, and

once you asked me to find
my replacement.

Cicero Avenue

There near the butcher's
shop, the man with a
serrated blade, hunkered,
good for bread cutting, sawing bones or

singing in darkness,
jaybird on a fence
waiting for an invitation.

There are death camps, places
like the backstreets of
Cicero. "Gimme some more."

Invitations like
jitterbugs, do-se-does, little
barn dances in Kansas,

tipped hats, shredded
sleeves, arm around
waist, dancing a blade

dance unseen, bathed
in dancing
lights.

After Apartheid

The welts, shirts stripped,
torn,
scars of Soreto banded on his chest,
back,
hell of black,
white, tempers ever
sounding:

"We'll get you for
this."
Written by exhalation,
flaying, somehow
dripping, we didn't doubt

they would,

being the highest part of the
escarpment intersecting
diamonds between
their teeth.

Infinity in Small Spaces

There's a wizard at the back door, he
moves like a sylph, beckoning with a gesture at the
one car in the driveway, the
turns in the empty bed, too
many sad songs played when
fast drums or slow steady rhythms
would be more useful, or a
drawing, etching, a painting by Chaval, and
we could be in one, rough tender strokes painted
on one tiny canvas framed in no
particular space. We've been singing the
ghosts of dreams, making patterns,
imperfect symmetry.

We're sightless as moles and
I'm not that bold, I'm
swinging on vines but expecting
lies, lies. There are things that hurt the most but often
make me feel alive. I'm smiling out of fear,
looking for, needing a phase change,

wishing on

the summer triangle, tangles in your hair, Vega,

Danube, Altair. I need a new

art form, lexicon, fortune. Words I said, "Half full," still
wait

for some substance to grace the glass. That old magic
flashes

brightly like wished for, and hope, but escapes like mist,

gossamer curtains flapping

unremembered in the end. What then?

The wizard, he

no longer performs.

Tell me what forever is not then,

show me the choices.

Dystopia

Anger can't dream, but
given the skeleton key
to the county asylum,
it's all that remains
of the Arbutus plucked from the yard,
or paraffin, for the whores
gasping with multiple
chains on their ankles.

On the corrugated roof
we stared with impudent eyes, dancing to tunes
played on the Melodica, tin
whole. No use saying the
horses wouldn't stand.

We were flogged while
counting out potatoes
In that queer hidden place
we called home.

Congruence

Into darkness, hope or not,
the silver glint of
a cleaver present.

I hold my hand
to a rodent cornered in
shadows, and there
he draws my blood.

Dust moles flow
from shattered window once
adored, dreams like
Déjà vu, so many promises.

A kite sails jet streams,
Red, silver against thought,
Scudding effortlessly, transforming as it dips,
Turns, tethered yet free.

Weeds choke up from
cracks in pavement. Is it evidence
of crumbled civilization?
Potholes in a senseless war?

We, like waves,
enhance or deplete
one another, accretion or
erosion changing our shores,
endlessly revisited, revised, and so,

ideologies separate us: sisters, brothers,
lovers; yet
dreams and anguish sometimes,
sometimes bond us together, and so
we go on.

Gun Control

When does it end,
reverberations shock implies,

recoil a simple pain
in blood flowing from
the bellies, brains,

children's screams, the endless torture;
those huddled living in dark
corners must endure, not

knowing when, if
the yellow bus at
three O'clock will arrive

automatically.

Choices

The air was broken
through hexagons of wire there,
in spicy shades of hemlock

when I fought. I didn't choose to leave home,
hold a gun, hold
back tears, understand sorrow.

I'm not a magic eight ball, not
a magic eight ball that
can close the eyes of fear.

his body leaked warmth, like
streaming out like
long jet necklaces looped

neatly over pegs,
splinters shaved off crutches,
cyclone of birds in distress.

with an upward cant of his head,
he called out a single aching
note of blood, pain, despair:
but that was before.

Not Angry
(For All the Wars Unwon)

Even the air is
broken, the bodies
uncovered, skeletal as
starving rats,
obviously gnawed on.

some still exude warmth
as if life continues to stream
out of rictus, orifices that might once
have held a smile, a
lover.

we didn't choose to hold
these guns, we didn't choose these
sudden tears as we look through
hexagonal cage wires of

myopic visions, coops disguised as
graves with a commander's
magic 8 ball in hand,
dogs digging furiously
to uncover cryptic versions
of what might never be truth.

we wouldn't know.

Strange Practices

The lie of fornication
like the shadows of
darkened races, burn from
behind, like a tainted,
fine red wine.

Finding the balance
on a tightrope bound
to vultures in flight,
some speaking in tongues,
courage only a cover, found.

Azrael knows
the waft of the tapestry and
the knights of the round, round
table, swords pricking their fall while
Iblis holds his sides, laughing.

An order, chains of sin, perversions.
No. Grinning like a Nihilist jester of malaise,
converted, convoluted, practices of
iconic choirs, ironic
dissatisfaction, all those inverted faces.

The confessions of a mad, mad woman.

A thousand cuts and curses,
flayed skin grasping the shape:
Seventh Book of Moses, guilt,

revealed by the Goat of Escape – Azazel.
Or was it simply stakes and rape?

Isabella singing on the Sabbath
of a blood spot in her eye (not hers),
punctuated by the torch, livid fire,
screams stabbed inch by inch
until there is no desire.

Fame, that vulture of history,
so many demons shaved for the
gravest mystery, or
diastolic dysfunction with
inverted corpses, rictus leering.

They eat their children with
Habeneros, ghosts in a
séance pickled in chaos: Castille, Aragón, *La Suprema;*
Reconquista applauding the dirge
of the fallen, forgotten Moors.

Tornidoros, Marranos,
Mariscos, Convertis, all the
creatures bellicose in
Roland's death scene, a victory of
reputation, a chasing of pigs.

They're still waiting for the bugle call.
The hunt goes on and on.

Seven and Ten

Abrasions of tenor, cat licks rough on
steel toe boots corrugated with
thighs opened wide, feline supine,
waiting on the lid of a dusty piano
at the corner bar. The boys look through, not at

into dreadlocks, dusky words that
swagger like a Shaka warrior in blue
denim, raging in herby barley grass,
pills and crushed white powder leading

crowds dancing with steel springs, their
Reebok hundred-dollar kicks, electric staccato
streetlights smashed, crazy magic, murders
of crows swirling overhead, the gunmetal

shots, gorge of dank alleyways: Diversey, Clark,
Wilson, Broadway. Chi-town sucked in macho moments;
graffiti spilling over peeling paint, pulsing music to
hip bones leading to another tenor scratching
a dirge laced with screams.

At Seaside Dock's

Ready to rumble
the seaside bird
divebombs atop
the philosopher, the astronomer,
the photographer's head
looking for its voice
where it fell out
some 32 years after the void.

Anger spins and twists
late into night
releasing those endorphins
resembling cold, heat,
verdant hell to senses.

There's a tale out there,
neither tragic nor
euphoric, while
a tiger sleeps blindfolded
permitting gentle hands to contour acts
and shapes into ecstasy sequestered
in places stripped of mindfulness.

Skin, vermillion, chafing
constant, as the sky splinters
into color.

Constructed Pain
(For Megan Holly)

Not a lot of snow, but
stark whiteness that entered my
lungs and filled them with a sharper
immediacy.

Memory is like that, sharp
or muted,
colors reflected up
from polished wooden floors
at unexpected times.

A sly little thing, stealer of
hearts, while hers, a
faltering tremor, weakened, the
back of my hand resting
on her cheek.

There were bridges to cross
I didn't recognize, over
gray streams mirroring gray
skies, hanging in wisps over
rooftops.

Holly and Mistletoe, the songs
that aired on the radio
spoken in tongues I couldn't
hear as we drove.

No damn cathedral with
spring flowers in the cold
December air brought relief,
comfort. No Phoenix would arise
from such a tiny grave.

Memories flare
like warm breath on a
cold winter day.

When

Did fire draw me in
fascination, burn a
welcome distraction

my brain filled with icy
resoluteness while
summer emerged in the
coreopsis of
my untended garden

did snow seem
absurd, an oriental carpet,
a symbol of objects collected,
anecdotes, experience
put aside

did I long to
swim into a setting
sun that no longer
held my significance

did monochrome grays
take over the spectrum,
and monochrome days
lead to monochrome nights

did adventure's alure stop:
still I've resisted,
still I embrace risk,
still continue on as

when
the poltergeist of my
imaginings emerged
from frowning tears,
shadows in the nave

no, I didn't find sensibility in
rapaciousness,
tinker sharpening blades
on a stone wheel that became
the archetypal villain I
thought I trusted in all those
books I read

did my vein draw
the needle in, smoke wraiths
surrounding my thoughts

When, then,
did I realize
you'd abandoned me?

Snapshots

There were tawdry linens scattered, a scuffed floor,
convenience of wisdom stepped on
in sweat.

Vistas of meat hanging, the butcher's
store, a corner man with scraggled beard asking
for more, pate glinting, toothing
a fag in the dusk. (Clouds of gnats buzzing
in haze.)

This scene: crowds clamoring
for the juggler dropping his fire
sticks, blaze contorting fissures, dry
air smoking up cries of adulation
torn from barking dogs.

Bottles gleam, neon over a score of
bowed heads, a Sunday afternoon of ripped
jeans, pilled sweaters, holy fishnets all

in a row drowning onion-garlic room, three
flights and a hallway to a one room walkup
on the next block with beer and vodka.
Laughter is gruff and frequent.

Or lights flicker, shadows grown
weak over pavement broken jutting up from
saplings cut from their prime, no apples
here, skylarks swimming through silty
chimneys, silhouettes against grainy
mauve, candles held high through a door, the
black robed men, hooded women following behind,
always behind, bathing hems, gripping
footstools.

No dimension, an etcetera, it's all defined
in dust, salt, the pictures our
mind kaleidoscopes at rest.

Four Deep

Blues, blacks, never expected
turn to red,
red as the chest spouts and
the man you
didn't know crumples.

Was it real that glint you
saw, ghost knife edge,
box cutter or

You never heard the
shot, only felt the recoil like
the recoil of a thousand
shots, but those were
in range.

Once you blew out
a kneecap. You wonder why
this bothers you. You saw
the man go down but
not again. In that
dank bar where you
drank numbness until you
could see again.

In the alley past Hollywood
under the El,
those sisters, undulating for the
uniform, when the Percocet wore
off, only isolation left, fleeting
moments, despair. But your
cock did its job. Yesterday.

A handicap? Backslaps, pain,
kneecaps ache, where
adrenalin pumped up
your throat. If breathing
was an issue, you did it
anyway, as if your body
derailed from your brain,

lizard brain, fight, flight,
fuck. There are static,
static voices disembodied
everywhere, telling you

Cyber blue, black
turned to red as the
glint of knife, maybe
boxcutter, ghost,
inflicts your rage in flashing
lights.

A Strange Lesson in Compromise

Expectations glitter like
diamonds far underground
destined for
favorable shadows
leaking like ink
through a crumbling wall's cracks
or on a Thursday,
interrupted by chanting
in the amygdala of a priest
doling duties,
duties to children, or sung
by a whale in New Zealand
while we skip and collide, then
take coal for an answer to
the cool end of
gemmed thoughts we renegotiate.

Discordant Music

Lute, basilisk, harpsichord,
music of distant shores, us,
ignoring ours

indigenous colored horizons,
drumming iron reds, violet seeds, blue,
green, black, our cloudy

thoughts free flowing,
spouting eruptions underground, unseen

tsunamis, waves that crest,
fugue like angry
lovers in a field of lotus, touched by

frequencies of amber, gold,
overtones fragrant as
violins, violas, that

raise the temperature of
a symphony dedicated
to the cadence
of a disturbing spring.

II
Undertones

That Day

When I dove off those
rocks at Wilmette Harbor
I knew the water would be
cold. I'm no fan of cold,
but that day
it had to be done, all
or nothing, no treading
water or dipping a toe in
to test the temperature.

Saturday Morning Near Boulder, Colorado

Fine mist drifted,
fog hinting at more
steady rain to come, the kind that
lasts for long, gray days.

In the clefts of rock, tansey,
chicory, thistle sprung, sprouting like
teparies, long roots fracturing
rock while mosses and lichens made
a landscape of shadows.

You sat on a plateau watching
pack rats dive into the midden behind
the shanty, abandoned now, pickings
pretty slim. I watched you smile before
you saw me.

A chorus of ravens erupted from pines,
crackling with
intelligence and humor. You
looked up then, green eyes flashing to
mine, canted your
head in salutation.

I knew in that moment exactly
what words rested in your thoughts,
because they were mine.

You were silent, and
I embraced us, that quiet knowing
that day you brought the rain.

Under Me

I had to bite just
then, just a little, to
be sure the divide was open
in case we crossed it.
Where What When

Skin crinkles at
the corners, but
its sharpness softens
the single sting.

There are no rainbows, no
pots of gold in this act.
At a cost, we learn each little
thing slowly.

I Remember You

If I whisper in
the night wind, you
It's because I know you
will hear me past
interlocking trinities, knots
that bound us in those
ides of March, then, now,
maybe forever. Sixteen,
a sprinkle of freckles, not much
else, reckless and full
of the empowerment of youth, me
set on a course of self-
destruction. You braided my
hair then, held it in a fist,
taught me to trust and surrender.

Spirit of Persephone

The music of footprints, distant shores,
basilic mixing harpsichord,
merging colors, rainbowing an
indigenous shore, drumming
iron reds, amber spackled violets, blues,
free-flowing thoughts, like
tsunami waves, lovers in a
field, lotus touched
fragrance, gold-tinged overtones in
violins, violas raising
temperatures, a symphony,
cadence dedicated to the arrival
of spring.

For Cousin Rita

The winds had no regard,
shifting from sultry to biting
hard that September afternoon, as Rita
sprawled on my lawn chair, shorts and
top a tease, skin like crème brûlée.

She called, voice smooth as
buttermilk, up from
the south, you know, low and
lilting vowels.

After sharing a mojito, I
stood in my kitchen and watched

this vignette through an open
kitchen window, kneading the
dough, hoping it would
rise.

At Dawn

And when I asked you
to teach me to fly,

you held my head
instead
to your chest,
grounded me
in negations,

sweet clover taking
over the green swept
lawns in the passage,

the Irish
freckles I counted
to the beat of
your heart

while you
slept.

Road Signs in the Forest

When going into the forest,
do we go deep?
Deep as thoughts on the
essence of dew clinging,
fronds drooping in dense
undergrowth? Thick like the skins
of pine?

Do we go in when the sun is
but a smudge, stars still
spackled against a violet
sky? Or midday, when shadows
cool our heated breath?

We tread there
lightly, letting earthy aromas lift
our steps, then look to the tops
of trees slightly swaying, let them
shift our perspective. Perhaps

we go later, afternoon or evening,
prepared to hear an owl
announce her intent, and see the vixen
creep through leaf
detritus. Watch silhouettes dance
against orange,

leave footprints
less frequently than our thoughts.

Tenuous Flight

There's a barn swallow
that swoops and pirouettes on air currents,
unaware until paired in dance
dreams, those romances written but unread,
ready on bookshelves, waiting like
dolphins about to spring from
the sea, or synchronized flights
in thought wanting freedom,

Pelican

Ripping the gauze out of
old wounds, a
single pelican folds her
wings on
dares, wishes, even lies,
pirouetting once, twice,
pauses with an airborne dancer's
grace, plunging to the
necessities the sea provides,
her elusive cry, silver
over breakers of foam,
indistinct haze, so many
desires.

Gently at Night

Night, taciturn darkness, the
thoughts of the old widow who
creeps into the church,
dressed in black, shadows

stretched over the inverted V between
her woman hips, eclipsing a younger
eagerness, nude breasts once
on display before a fireplace,

crushed by a set of
tracks, needles hollow, still,
the ambush succeeds lost time,
memory, meaning,

saturated in stolen breath.
She grasps the scattered
fragments, genuflects, and
places the pieces back gently, in
darkness.

Change

You slept on while I,
riding across the
backbone of the Midwest watched,
hating the time spent looking at
checkerboard fields undulate out the window,
redundant, the same, fearing your
silence, fidgeting while you slept on

the train
was a deception in rhythm, pacifying
algorithm, belying the care and courage we
needed to get past, to another
side. Acres of living stretched before us, hope in
this one sunset, cooling sky, contrails
bisecting deep blues, dark shadows as dusk
took over and the switchbacks in the mountains
patterned purple and gray, eagles circling high
above, already the scent of desert, dry, with
Saguaro Cacti standing sentinel and judging

our approach before we arrived. So many generations
of silence, and I couldn't help but need a sound,
shake you to share the wonder of
a patch of Amaranth in such an unexpected
place, before the midnight dark took over
and forgiveness was no longer
flexed in the wind's secrets
as we rushed by.

Sunday Hymn

He was that youth with blurred lines between
childhood and adult: tall, thin, loose of limb, gangly, one
might say. if one saw him, his wide brown eyes, long
tawny curls below the chin, one might think dangerously

when the bells pealed from St. Mary Sunday
morning, at first, we didn't really notice,
sitting in our own peacock finery,
the sacrosanct pew on the third to the
left that somehow, we had come
to understand was his, but no one
knew his name, knew where
he was from.

we all assumed someone else
should know if he came from
Sheridan or Broadway Avenue,
from across the El tracks where the hookers
plied their trade, or from the

steel and glass high-rises that
bordered the lake. someone else would
know that, sure, something about him,
with his loose tattered jeans and lanky
demeanor.

that Sunday in July, we
traded glances over the
empty place he once occupied, quickly
finding other interests, looking away, and
if the conversation was just a little
bit louder, more forced, no one was
about to say. We fanned our faces
in the heat.

when he disappeared, he became
known to us: a silence
crept into the hearts of some of
those parishioners who quietly
collected coins, bills, who
learned a liturgy unspoken: of
indifference, the scourge of conscience,
but had not planned to succumb so
willingly, until we

heard about it on the 10 o'clock news.

In Place

On this day,
this day we shelter
from touch, contagion
in place, sending virtual
hugs, elbow bumping behind
masks, gloves, emptying
shelves of toilet paper, canned goods,
frozen entrees. So,
so we can have reassurance in the
quantity of our hoarding,
lording a larder past full. No surprise
here. Always has it been
thus, when disaster loomed. Greed or
survival instinct? Amygdala
suspended. And yet, and yet there are
pockets of kindness, community,
sharing and warmth. Not everyone shelters
from the community of humanity.
Can one thought or poem change mass

fear? Like the proverbial butterfly wings
that raise a storm? When the curses escaped
Pandora's Box, they say hope remained. Always
there is hope, one act of kindness, one
poem at a time.

Segway

When I'm undone
by the movement of tides,
shifting clouds, mirrors of

dances, or swiftly scribing
pens, oracles flanging
adverbs like birds

startled by sudden
winds or fish that
leap like ballerinas or

redundant idioms, I need
to ask, "Where does this
go when I am done?"

The hook writes (rights?)
left, and who IS Lilly, anyway?

We dream of wraiths or
wraiths dreaming of us
in nocturnal blindness
as we dig holes and then fill them.

Prize

This November morning,
cold hangover from an
insolent hunter's moon, too bright, too
much, making a lie of the
night, shadows all that much blacker
for it until

predawn paints a fiction of peace
red as maple leaves, mostly fallen and soon
turned to haze, indistinct grays
subverting twilight, crystals in
every breath, a fog that covers

flashes of white: the stillness of
phantom fox, doe, the
damp decay coruscating gold in
lattices of vine, evergreen, maple,
oak and birch, smell of loam, the
near naked foliage hardly camouflage

above, the hunter cocks, eye, finger
experienced, motionless in the spit
of an ancient elm, silence pondering
a small flash of reflected glass as
the doe pauses, one slender hoof lifted delicately, *en pointe*
the fox already gone, melted into junipers

she lifts her head, nose aquiver, all
tawny, speckled with the last vestige of youth
and knows, as only instinct can, resigned to a fate
regret only tarnishes

the gray-green man at last presses
his finger and braces against recoil, a perfect
shot to the hart's neck:
reverberations, ricochets, startled echoes sound
as the buck on the hill gracelessly falls
as the hunter intended:
twelve-point trophy, a prize no
longer lover, empty eyes, such
beast that he was, watching over her:

sacrifice without witness, not quite selfless,
not quite guessed, relief a lie for those who'd survive

another day in an unremarkable
forest on a crisp November morning
that took a heart carved, still beating,

raised eagerly to a hunter's lips,
smiling in a
remarkable sunrise.

Thorns

I run my wrists along
rose stems, barely feeling
the trickle of pain, red welts
raised on my inner skin,
like memories that surface
and haunt. The Hurt.

Once we had
the Bahá'i Temple, a deserted beach,
Winnetka, in Illinois.
I dove into the cold lake water
just to prove my freedom, but
freedom was being with
you that day.

We had smiles and
laughter, hand-in-hand jousting
with words, words that became
us, survivors as we were of
sickness, soreness, abuse and
love ill-spent. We didn't tell all
our secrets then, we sequestered away

what didn't fit our plans
to walk, walk together down
Hermitage, Olive, Paulina,
Clark Street in Chicago.

We grew together then,
lying on the floor of an old antique store
filled with music. On
inhalation, we formed streams of words,
creative evidence of us
as we stroked storied dreams
from each other.

"Someday," you said, and I
turned and sighed. You pulled me against
you, wrapped your arms around me,
curled up against my
back. Later, you took the el south
while I dusted the books you'd wrote and
left behind.

My electric typewriter, near antique,
whirred and clacked, trying in vain
to catch my thoughts as I tried to capture
both the here of you, the absence of you, and the
emptiness of my nights without you

until it was gone, another
artifact stolen in the business of
decisions, expectations, situations
we never chose, or chose
blindfolded.

You never did see the stars
like I did, even before I knew
their names. Perhaps our constellations
were tenuous, even then.

There's a loneliness about winter, and
those red roses are now black and
brittle against the new fallen snow. I never knew
that could happen

so I turn my wrists inward, as if
bound in handcuffs, and watch
beads of blood rise up, listening,
only listening, clasping

as an empty wind sighs
a song, a tune, lyrics, and rhythm
I might remember
from before. I want
to hurt somehow, more intensely.

Dreamer
(For Nova)

She drifts, one foot
falling over the edge of
the cot like a slender vine
and dreams, slipping

down rabbit holes,
eating cabbages with kings,
walruses, metamorphosing
in my down cocoon. There are
sharks out there, lightly
resting atop silver seas, like
dragonflies, so many

jewels between their
teeth. Hands upraised, she
grasps the iron headboard,
REM permutations
congregate like spurious children's
wisdom, coming out
of nowhere, nowhere to go,

long dark lashes spilling into
a slight smile, the stories we've
shared,

while feathers whip
her hair, glass of brandy on the
table not quite empty, not quite
full, pulsing sanger in her veins as
she sleeps; as I watch.

Singing Down the Rain

Side by side
on the rocks of
Wilmette Harbor, watching
gray-green clouds broil in, we
made no sound that summer day
we sang down the rain.

Remember

Take me down that
dusted road again, dappled
with cloud shadow, maple
and elm leaves
dancing in spirals, us breathing
evergreen punctuations.

No words spoken, no
ringtones,
only wind sighs,
bird conversation, our synchronized
footfalls. A monarch settled on
your shoulder then as we clasped hands
in quiet wonder.

Starlings

This is NOT about you,
or carnal thoughts that
roil and wreck my
everyday composure:

aphorisms elephants
might spout at one another
in their intelligent discourse
take up my days or

fractus clouds in an
iridescent sky or

convective roils
of dreams like
flocks of starlings

that burst into flight and
turn synchronically on
a single idea

and I remember some
birds are earthbound:

those that can fly
do so with impudence
high above misfortune,

cobblestone, concrete,
asphalt, ash

with forward facing eyes,
canines in disguise

and you and I.

Batteries

I'm shattered as I
collide once again: you,
fight dried up like seaweed on the beach,
opaque mask an impenetrable deep
darkness, an indelible
guilt stain, Rorschach blot
heaving on waves
out of control.

What conductor is it that
passes the charge
through sinews and skin,
your words tattooed,
catacombed like tiny
incisions, opened, salted anew
each time I begin
to heal?

Once the sun danced on a galleon,
spray splattered, simple
arithmetic in stark
musculature, I fell into

caskets, bones
scattered on the seabed, skulls
hollow-eyed, inviting fish to dart in.

Outliers

It could have been the sidereal moon
got them dancing, those Pekingese with
those Labradors, side by side, the meadow
full of larkspur dotting the new green, gray-green
in shadow. Yellow caged birds watched from the veranda,
mesh steel to grind upon, red peels of paint slowly
unraveling from the walls. "I love dogs," from within.
"I'm tired," an old voice replied.
"Dogs make me happy!"
"Sam was a horrible dog."
"I love dogs," came the lilting voice, "because dogs love
everyone." Slowly,
a cold fog crept in, the birds began to shiver. Those canines,
though,
those canines simply bared their teeth, then,
began to dance in earnest.

Blindfolded

How did it go,
that song we liked
to hear? Something
about reasons,
canted toward a silent lake,
view of reminiscence
fast forwarded to
streets bordered by
single family houses all
manicured, silent windows
like accusing eyes,
gray and white,
dappled in sameness. We
couldn't hear the words
over the engine as
we turned on a red,
veering through town,
driving accusations 'till we
no longer could turn right back
around – crashing.
The moment was just so.
We couldn't see.

Greed

The Umthakathi came
to examine your disease, toe
blister just a symptom of
greed, vaporous gray
blanket, tempest of blind
to need, the needs of others. You
laughed, indeed, at the willingness of others
to surrender their goods, hard earned, trusting you.

As the frogs grew silent, he
said, "Put it on the braai, for all our
good, the sick sick
needs cutting." And then
he did.

Iberian Pigs

To make a great
ham, kill the pigs
that eat acorns

black feet, black
skin, and pretend they
are free to go

dance flamenco or
tango with the devil's
fireworks, express a
virulent grudge

against the
Poyoyo and Montchengos
and the men who
hide steel behind
their smiles

or the Defense Ministry that
always checks the
banding of Black
Footed Pigs, peering under
rocks, logs, wherever life
comes from the dark

places where they
crawl into disbelief, those

pigs, busy digging
their own hollow deaths,
imprinted as they are, eating acorns.

No exit from the shining knives
watching, the grinning masters
awaiting the apathy pigs
always have when fat and feeling
grand. No sorrow then, only screams
when even breathing

is not enough.

Transport (Berlin)

I hear your whispered lyrics,
your glass harmonics, the brittle
ellipses standing on the
tracks of the U-Bahn in
July. Raspberry Basil
ice cream on the double decker
bus # 29, rocking through
Reichpietschufer and
Vander Heydt Gretße
gets me somewhere.
Know I'm often lost, but

sometimes, (when
silence is a curse you've forced, and I buck
those cautious maps and the
directions of others) I
hop on, hop off, a
seeker at the underpass, drawn to the
Hibernian, digging among worn
dusty books for comfort, knowing, knowing,
I'm not better than that.

Sometimes, I am found.

Let's Talk

Let's talk about
Reaching the event horizon,
And slipping over it,
Stretching, and then stretching some more,
Through possibilities, and time,
Hoping to grow up someday and understand.

Me: so afraid to reach for the singularity
That might only be a dead star, and not really knowing if
A quasar might release
All the hopes and dreams
In the eleven dimensions
I hold in the Universe of my mind.

Let's talk about
The Fibonacci Sequence
Russell's Paradox,
The Enigma Code,
Pascal's Triangle,
Turing's Morphogenesis,
Reaction Diffusion,
And Fractals.

And why

A bipolar nebula looks just like

A butterfly,

And a bullfrog tadpole looks just like a human male's sperm.

And why a woman might despair and hunger for her own creations.

A cumulus cloud looks like a mushroom,

And a nerve cell and a starfish have pretty much the same pattern as my brain tissue.

Let's talk about

A web of existence that may or may not include

A multiverse,

Where there are no limits,

And hope is present.

Finally, let's talk about If

The desire for soft slow licks to taste

The salty sweet musk of existence

Ever fades.